APZ 273

Charles Stein

Poems and Glyphs

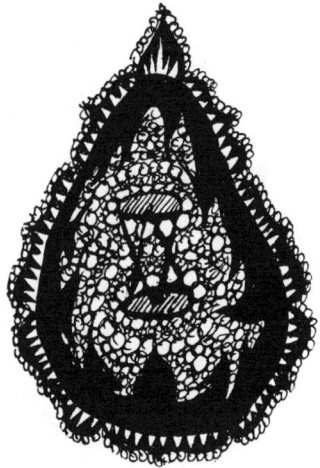

Io Books, Plainfield, Vermont, 1973

POEMS AND GLYPHS

CONTENTS

All drawings, cut-outs, and photographs (of
the Cumulus) are by the author.

PREFACE by Richard Grossinger

Last fall, while teaching a course on poetry, I put together an ethnographic and thematic chart of my own hypothetical core of modern American literature. Initially, I distinguished three major poetic loci and transmissions: Bay Area poetry, the so-called Beat poetry, and the Black Mountain poetry. Each of these groups has a visible energy source: Robert Duncan in San Francisco, Allen Ginsberg for the Beats, and Charles Olson at Black Mountain; and each of these figures is linked up with other major figures in the transmission of poetic themes and forms in the English language: Duncan with Blake, Dante, H.D., and the romantic and classical traditions; Ginsberg with Blake, Whitman, and William Carlos Williams; and Olson with Pound, Williams, and the mythic and historical traditions. There is obvious overlap among the groups, both in influences generative to them and dynamic interaction between them; many individuals combine groups, and others oscillate, showing varying connections at different times, often for accidental and idiosyncratic reasons. These are not schools; they are like the archetypal foci of energy most susceptible to being brought into formal realization in our present time. If we imagine three trunks in the ground, the fact is that the branches twist together into a single tree, and we are able to distinguish only different original sources of nourishment.

Among the San Francisco poets I listed, for divergent reasons, Duncan, Spicer, Blaser, Kyger, Levertov, Meltzer, McClure, Antoninus, Dull; they are very much spread across the whole West Coast (and elsewhere, of course, too), with centers in Bolinas, Vancouver, and Toronto. For the Beats: Ginsberg, Snyder, Kerouac, Petersen, Montgomery, Orlovsky, Ferlinghetti. For Black Mountain: Olson, Dorn, Creeley, Dawson (in prose), Wieners, and Blackburn (via Creeley via Pound), with a North Carolina offshoot under Jonathan Williams, including Metcalf and LeRoi Jones among others, for reasons having substantially to do with publishing.

The most immediately-startling thing about this chart was that it appeared to omit (or deflect) the one sector of things in which I would include myself. It is true that I could have extended the section out from Black Mountain, but I chose instead to map a fourth group, with Robert Kelly at the head and including Wakoski, Rothenberg, Irby, Oppenheimer, Eshleman, Enslin, and indirectly others, like Sorrentino and Sanders, the obvious anomaly being Kelly's age and national stature in comparison with the other three charismatic figures, but this is a trivial and relative matter if there are other issues of substance.

The connection between this group and Black Mountain is basic and clear, and is typified in the work and movements of three people. Paul Blackburn could be considered either a Black Mountain poet via his direct involvement with Pound and his early correspondence with Creeley or a member of the Kelly-group via his New York location and close relation to Kelly and early Kelly publishing ventures. After Olson's move to Gloucester, Gerrit Lansing is a close communicant of both him and Kelly on spiritual and historical issues very dear to all three of them. And, thirdly, Stan Brakhage, the film-maker, has combined the Kelly and Olson concerns in a massive visual transformation. Kelly himself had a significant friendship with Olson, but the men worked out from one another rather than towards.

Of the poets mentioned above, only three, Enslin, Irby, and Lansing, have been unambiguously involved in the concerns that Kelly's work centers. The others have gone their own ways and have successfully defined more intermediate positions, all of them, from my vantage, ultimately compromises of Kelly-articulated material. I find myself right in the center of a group of my contemporaries that seems to arise with its own force and intelligence right in the midst of the Kelly field. It has no head, but insofar as three of us are involved directly, it is literally triple-headed, with everyone's work (for everyone else) peculiarly inclusive and complete given their own limitations. The three are myself, Charles Stein (whom I met in high school), and Harvey Bialy (whom Stein met thru Robert Kelly and whom I met when he came with Stein on a visit to Amherst my third year there). Recently George Quasha has been right in the center of this too, and others, including Tom Meyer, Lindy Hough, Bruce McClelland, Linda Parker, and Jonathan Greene, have connections.

The Beats, the Bay Area poets, the Black Mountain people, and our own group are all concerned with matters of consciousness, vision, prophecy, cosmology, geography, etc., few of which are even peripheral to academy poetry in America, which is more involved in description, emotional reality, wit, and political rationalism. Yet there are differences, not always easily described. The Beats sought to make America livable, and they discovered, in its present visible state, the rest of the world. They lived, as best they could, a vision (variously Buddhist, Marxist, and American Indian), and made their migrations and very bodies the source of a dramatic and mythological history of our time. They were like wandering saints who humanized America, and we owe them much of our present social ease and grace. The San Francisco poets, perhaps for being West Coast urban and closer to the Orient and the American West in some literal sense, were less migratory, and less originally American. In some of them a Western World hermeticism and mystery poetry is brought into being directly from the contact of Western tradition with the proto-Western and the non-Western. They were like reincarnated literary giants who had lived and travelled in other times and were now recovering their own archetypes, fairy tales, and histories. The Black Mountain people had various involvements including the mythological recovery of history, the recovery of myth, the individual as the written record of cosmology, phenomenology, the Whiteheadian process universe, and astronomy-astrology as a record of time. Olson's involvement in history and economics, via Pound, formed a crucial center against which many of the other concerns were located. The opening lines of Don Byrd's thesis on Olson are relevant here:

"Charles Olson is in an intellectual tradition which has been the cause of much discomfort in the twentieth century, much more discomfort than the existentialist tradition which has devoted itself to arousing awareness of the human 'predicament' which brings anguish at every turn. Unlike the existentialists, who measure life by some ideal footrule and find it lacking, Olson answers to Freud and Jung, Whitehead and the Cambridge anthropologists, Ezra Pound, D.H. Lawrence, and William Carlos Williams. Their gift, though it has not been graciously received, is testimony to the possibilities of *largeness* in thought and action, which the desiccated things human beings have allowed themselves to become, fear and suppress. These men have cleared space for a vision of man, conditioned, no doubt, by the earth and the limits it places on

4

meaning and action, but which, at the same time, allows access to a source of energy larger and more useful than any the 'official' culture offers or the existentialists have been able to imagine." [D. J. Byrd: *Charles Olson's Maximus: An Introduction*, 1970].

These statements tie in directly with Kelly. As a Mediaevalist he has been more intimately in touch with occult sciences and the history of magic. Whereas Olson derived certain license from Hesiod and the Greeks, and John Smith and the American settlers, as joint beginnings of our time, Kelly has come to his work more as a daily spiritual exercise, bringing the poem forth as human mediation between its own sphere of sensory contact and those spheres initiatory to it. The poet, like alchemist or magus (and more recently, like scientist) is both transformer of original cosmic material and contact with angellic and natural agencies. Kelly's explorations have grounded his work at various times in alchemy, astrology, traditionary wisdom, Islam, the East, as well as science, mathematics, genetics, astronomy, geology, history, etc. His engagement with these is not primarily scholarly, for he has made other texts over into the body of his text. Just about everyone in the fourth group is either directly touched by these concerns or touched by Kelly as a person and artist. It is not that he has appropriated this territory exclusively, but he has given it its widest articulation and most dynamic integration with our present human condition. Insofar as there is a group centered here, this preface is the first occasion on which *Io* has been cited as the journal born in that center. Yet, if it has been the voice of these people, it has never been so exclusively or self-consciously, or literarily, which would have been an undermining of the very principles and conditions it has sought to explore.

Those who have remained closest to Kelly's concerns have also been notably unambitious in developing poetic egos or pushing and publishing their work. Stein and Bialy, for instance, are not particularly well published because other things have, properly, come first, not before the work but before the advancing of the work and a social engagement with its possibilities. Bialy is a biochemist and research scientist, with a deep involvement in magic, whose primary work is still his writing. Stein is a musician and artist, a longtime student of yoga, whose writing is his articulation of rhythms in his life.

Will Petersen said to me recently (about a certain American poet in Japan who said his occupation was "poet"): "In my day that was just something you didn't do. You were a carpenter or a gas station attendant; you might be an artist or poet, but that was on the side. If you were going to claim it you better have your dukes up."

In the Kelly genre there is no such social embarrassment, but to make claims about being a poet and to develop a social persona around it is to put one's self in a dangerous relation with those muses and sources of power that give poets insight. And one literally does have their dukes up and is doing more fighting than writing if publishing comes before putting one's self humbly at the disposal of higher energies who, in fact, become the voices of the poems. I will let Charles Stein talk on a few of these things in order to clarify their relation to his own history:

"The first poems that I remember were in Niswender's class, and

5

they were Ariel's Song "Full Fathom Five" from *The Tempest*, which he did
a whole sound analysis of (he was talking about technical things like
assonance and so forth) and "Mending Wall" by Robert Frost. That had
very peculiar lines. The way he bends language and all for someone
who's never read any poetry is very startling. "Something there is
that/Does not love a wall" was very far-out for me and it started from
go a kind of interest in language. Then someone gave me *Howl* to read
and it knocked me out. It was more just the content and intensity of
it.

I went to camp, and we used to sit under oak trees and read each
others' poems, and we were also reading Ferlinghetti and e.e. cummings
and Lorca and William Carlos Williams. Eric Felderman went to that
camp, and Jonathan Greene was there also, and Jonathan's first year at
Bard, which would have been about 1960, he spent his winter semester
typing for Larry Eigner, and when I went up there to visit him, we
went to see Olson, and boom! there was Olson. I had seen a poem of his;
I think it was "The Lordly and Isolate Satyrs," at a Wesleyan Poetry
Conference thing and hadn't had much interest in it, and it was really
sometime, maybe a year, after that, that I was reading Olson and trying
to write like that. Then Duncan and trying to write like that, and
Creeley and trying to write like that. Really Jonathan was into those
people more intensely than I was at that time. I met Kelly in June of
1960. Jonathan was in Armand Schwerner's study hall at Barnard, and it
was Schwerner who brought us down to this place where they were all
reading, and I was supposed to play music for their poetry reading. I
sat in the window and played on a flute and a saxophone without blowing
into them, just making noises on them on the keys, and being freaked
out by it.

When Kelly went to Bard I used to go visit Jonathan and together
we'd go to visit Kelly. I don't think I got interested in his poetry
until I was in college. And then, being around him constantly, his
stuff was always in my ear. But I had a very ambiguous attitude towards
it because there was much of me that was very conservative. I hadn't
given up the idea that what you ought to be doing really was writing
formal verse and I would be constantly relapsing into experiments wri-
ting blank verse and doing formal translations. In a sense Robert
Lowell broke that because when he wrote *Life Studies* I didn't know that
it was broken-up couplets as he later said. It sounded like free verse
to me. After that I wasn't really interested in writing formal verse.

What was important in Kelly was the tension that writing poetry
had something to do with the way you lived your life, that in some way
the highest activity of your mind was what occurred when you were wri-
ting, that you couldn't do better than that, and that in some way the
rest had better be subordinated to it because otherwise you were just
wasting your energy and your time. That's always been partly believed
in me. When I was in B.O.T.A. [Builders of the Adytum] I was resisting
that notion intensely and feeling very strongly that it wasn't so, that
poetry was just one of the things one did; and your relation to God and
the Universe was your relation to God and the Universe. Poetry was nice
but you couldn't take it as the whole thing. The disappointment after
a while with the possibility of identifying with some religious or
political (or in fact any kind of intellectual) order other than a

poetic one has left me with feelings pretty similar to Kelly's: that indeed fundamental activity takes place in writing, and though I find great use for meditating (and every other kind of consciousness experiment), I return to writing to accomplish that activity. What I had felt all along was that somehow it was too easy to say that you just had to write, that such a choice would leave you with an empty writing. I felt that you had to back up the writing by at least doing the things that you were saying. I mean that if, in poetry, you claim that you have the alchemical work, which is the external correlate to the realization of the highest human potential, you better really be realizing higest human potential. The lives of the poets I knew did not really seem to be that, nor did Kelly's. He seemed very smart and had a way of getting around any objections that you had to his way of life, but somehow you didn't feel that you could take him as a master of life. Of course, at this point I don't feel that it's necessary to do that. I'm not out comparing people's modes of life. And it was also true that everybody who was claiming to be a master of life in all those other terms had similar kinds of shortcomings. I'm no longer interested in perfection in that way. Nor do I have a particular definition of what the full realization of human potential or the best possible use of the mind would be, but I have a very concrete sense of my own activity and what's fruitful and what processes are rich."

Kelly's influence is neither singular nor direct. Since Gerrit Lansing, Ken Irby, George Quasha, Harvey Bialy, Chuck Stein, and I are all influenced in important ways by Kelly, and yet are making similar and synchronous discoveries on our own, it is not always clear where any theme arises, if in fact it arises in any one place. We are all in contact within a certain psychological and psychic framework. Stein explains some of his own connections:

Gerrit Lansing: "I met him not too long after I started getting friendly with Kelly. Gerrit always occupied the polar position that poetry was subsidiary to one's spiritual or magical work and that the making of the poem had a specific function in terms of self-creation, and no relation to history or public or anything of the kind. I mean in that sense that he had none of Kelly's Christian concern or Poundian concern with being publically committed, and he simply reinforced my other interests, my interests in meditation and other related practices. At the point that I was experiencing a doctrinal line from Kelly, Gerrit would be giving me the opposite, and he was at least as strong a person, so in terms of influence it made me tow the line between them. You asked me for Gerrit's interests. Magic, that's his interest. Cooking. Plants. Herbs. All literature; he's certainly one of the great readers of a whole range of subjects. Jungian psychology. Jungian anthropology. Jungian thought with all of its antecedents, i.e., history of religion, alchemy, magic in the West, plus an incredible erudition on the arcane events of American history, arcane not only in the sense of the inner interstices of what actually happened but the either real or fantasized occult implications of the spiritualist-magical events on the inner contours of American history."

Harvey Bialy: "Harvey has given me some gestures and an intensity of rhythmical energy of a certain kind; many of the poems in this book, particularly the poems called "Buzz Saws," are written out of the ener-

gy of playing music with him (he plays the drums and I play the alto
sax). Harvey's total love affair with spade America and jazz and nasti-
ness, underworld dope America and the romance of evil, has gotten me as
near to it as I want to get. At the same time I was getting into poetry
and mysticism and meditation I was getting into jazz. In talking about
meditation and poetry I have emphasized the importance of time, but we
could just as well talk about music and different kinds of representa-
tions of time in different music, certainly in free jazz. The approach
to time in Ornette Coleman, Albert Ayler, Cecil Taylor, and some of
Coltrane is close to where I'd like to think my attitude is. Basically
what free jazz does to the metrical structure of classical jazz, pre-
Ornette Coleman jazz, is to tighten the interval of the minimal beat
such that you can have a gigantic variety of possible figures laid down
over a very tight grid; that minimalization of their interval, of
tightening up the rhythm, affords one a field in which it's possible to
program many many many more aspects of bodily rhythms into the rhythmical
field, and to give a much wider range and variety of forms. I was into
that more as a spectator until I started playing with Harvey; he picked
it up from Moffit, with whom he played, and he had that charge as a
technician and as a drummer. That works in with meditation too, that
feeling of attention to the tightest interval. Harvey's also very good
on numbers, languages, the histories of numbers plus the whole Jungian
and Levi-Straussian question of the dominant numerical structures that
determine any given cosmology: whether it's a cosmology of one or two or
three or four or five, and the different kinds of worlds that are made
possible by those basic paradigms."
      George Quasha: "I've only been friendly with George for a year and
a half, but in some ways it's like playing back all the years of con-
versation with Kelly, only with a peer. Many of the things that were in
my head from that time have come up again in another context. Quasha is
very much into the vision of the poetic process as spiritual process,
from Blake, also the visionary process, the prophetic process. In Soma-
poetics, his big poem for the last year and a half, his conception is to
permit as many different kinds of writing as he's ever considered to
operate in the field that the poem creates so that the highest level of
content is an exposition of language itself. How do you on the one hand
write nondramatic poetry which doesn't create characters, on the other
hand not create narrative dramatic psychomachia characters as Dorn does?
What Quasha does is to let the most physical aspect of language, i.e.,
the timing of repetitions, form the structural field in which every dif-
ferent kind of language plays: people speaking, descriptive things, imi-
tations of different kinds of things, miracle things, constantly cutting
it, constantly throwing every given process up against its opposite,
letting it twist and then throwing it opposite that. This is relevant
for me certainly in the "Buzz Saws" where the intellectual idea is also
to objectify the language until you're using your own speaking voice to
do your own singing, your own speaking even while the effect of the poem
is a step back from that. Where Harvey uses the tight interval jazz
drumming of Charlie Moffit to be the physical, Quasha uses the repeti-
tion and the actual occurrence of things as the physical mode for per-
mitting his voice to be both a voice and a picture of the voice. I do
that in the "Buzz Saws" by having an actual physical beat moving under
the poem, like a jazz technique: very tight and not simply revealed in

what would be called the metrical structure. The actual driving energy of it is not a counting of syllables or a placing of accents; it's a keeping of an unstated rhythmical pulse, on top of which the poem occurs; that is, there's both a speaker and a nonspeaker at the same time. I tink that that process, of letting the voice be itself and at the same time providing a context which objectifies it, is another thing which is very directly related to meditation, particularly Buddhist meditation, where the process doesn't involve an attempt to control thought or direct it in particular channels but to create a space in which whatever is occurring simply occurs, with the transformation occasioned by the space in which it occurs.

Duncan is also counting beats underneath the rhythm that are not accents and not anything like metrical forms or accents or lengths of syllables, but he's got an actual series of contrapuntal bodily pulses on top of which the writing is done. Both the voices that Duncan represents and the underlying rhythmical structure that he uses are different than what Quasha, or Bialy, or I are involved in, but the mode is related. Finally, Quasha's pushing me constantly that the mappings of all these connections between us should be made as clear as possible and that we should explore some of the amoebal connections that exist in reality."

Richard Grossinger: "In some ways your anthropological concerns and your actually doing the geographical work that Olson lays down has been very important for me. Also, your cosmology has created a context for mine. When I was reading *Ogotemmeli* and building my pile, *Io* and the many conversations with you were as present as anything else."

Charles Stein was born in New York City on August 23, 1944. By the time I met him, at Horace Mann, he was already involved in music, drawing, and yoga; he was a good baseball player and on the school bowling team. Soon after, he got involved in poetry, but even before that he was deeply engaged in reading, literature, philosophy, politics, and history. Chuck, together with Bob Alpert, James Polachek, and a few others, formed a kind of floating salon. There was more energy than style involved. They made the school into an intellectual hotbed, and previously quiet and mysterious teachers turned out to have provocative and esoteric backgrounds, and were drawn into the conversations on subjects they probably never dreamed they would discuss for the rest of their days. The issues of life and the universe were debated daily, in class, during lunch, between classes, with incredibly strong and desperate thrusts of enthusiasm and commitment. Polachek was a musician and brilliant student who is now in Far Eastern Studies at Berkeley after doing Chinese at Harvard. Alpert was a Marxist and social humanist who now teaches school at Monterrey after doing early English literature at Harvard and Berkeley. Others included Erwin Morton, a mathematical genius, Bob Karlan, who became heavily involved in I Ching and tarot right after Horace Mann, plus those in other classes involved in film, American history, Spanish literature, Chinese politics, metaphysical logic, etc. Chuck experienced a fluency and articulation in this world of ideas at a very young age, and it sometimes strikes me that because of this, he has been moving since then toward the spaces beyond the usual articulate voice.

The Horace Mann group was very powerful and influential in our lives. Chuck expressed it well when he said, recently, of the way in which we were taught people like Melville and Stephen Crane and Willa Cather: "They were initiations into exactly the things they were meant to be initiations into, but they were not initiations into those books as they were intended." I saw Polachek recently for the first time in years, and he wrote me in a letter:

"Chuck initiated the Resistance. Right there, in our midst, at Horace Mann, it happened; can you imagine the potential of putting us together in the same building for six years, five days a week? What Marx saw happening in the factories but which never has."

Much of my image of Chuck comes from these times, the part of the image in fact that he is most uneasy about my including in here: a kind of purposely tattered quixotic magus, showing up at school each day and doing excellent work in the school's terms while committing subtle outrages on the system: photographed for the yearbook in the garbage can, lying down before the assembly raving, "They're all madmen in there. Don't go in!" to the startled underclassmen; he blames Polachek for conducting the profane mass over the spaghetti in the dining hall when our formidable history professor was communicating with macho awe the mysteries of the Mediaeval Church. I report all this as an outsider.

When the class graduated (Chuck receiving the Honors award in creative writing), he went to Columbia to study Greek. He says:

"I took Greek because I very arrogantly didn't want to take English courses and have to confront academic attitudes towards poetry. Kelly was constantly emphasizing that it was stupid to do in college what you could do on your own and that you could use the occasion of being in a University to learn something you couldn't do on your own. I had been reading Pound since high school and Pound is adamant on the importance of Homer and Sappho. Its use to me has been manyfold: one, some familiarity with an alternative to English prosody, that is, the quantitative metric, which I never understood in Latin but found in Greek poets like Sappho and Archilochus and Homer as a whole other kind of metrical possibility, more interesting than the traditional English structures. There is also Olson's whole take on the importance of the moment of Greek philosophy, of Parataxis and Homer as an "in" on the history of Western civilization, which I keep redoing in many ways, like reading Steiner now. Also the heavy Greek tragedy stuff has a place in my head."

While at Columbia Chuck visited Kelly, Lansing, Olson, and Duncan, and edited one issue (1964) of a magazine called *Aion*. "I was doing Gerrit's and Kelly's project for them, and this was my own initiation into their world." The issue included: Kelly, Lansing, Duncan, Jonathan Greene, Stein, Zosimos translated by Stein, and Crowley. The preface said:

"*Aion* is a Journal of the Traditionary Sciences which, in C. G. Jung's phrase, include "Researches into the Phenomeology of Self as understood in Alchemy, Astrology, Ceremonial Magic and related disciplines.

Aion will serve as an exchange between purely "Occult" and other concerns; literary, historical, scientific; thus, texts from, essays about, accounts of, poems out of.

Aion will be as open as possible in terms of doctrine, operating with few assumptions other than that these concerns are relevant now.

10

We would hope to effect an opening of the "occult" to influences from without - at least an opening of what is already public to intelligent examination as well as a presentation of "occult" material in a more intellectually palatable form than in publications now out and correspondence courses generally available."

After Columbia, Stein went on in Comparative Literature at NYU, but dropped out pretty quickly and took a nine to five job. He worked for *True Romance* and *True Experience* and then edited a master buying guide for a photo trade magazine. After a year of that he went back to school at Hunter and taught at Pace College. Finally, after Olson's death, he moved out of the New York area on a permanent basis for the first time and entered the graduate program in English at the University of Connecticut at Storrs (where Olson's papers have been purchased by the library). He is completing his PhD. with a thesis on Olson.

"At Hunter I was mostly interested in Seventeenth Century and Metaphysical poetry. But generally, for the first time, I got into learning the kind of anthropo-intellectual history of the various periods of English literature. At Storrs I simply got hung on reading English poetry, all of it. I read Browning and Tennyson, and there the development of late light verse is so intricate you can literally lay down any accent on it; you can read it in a bold American accent and it makes perfect sense. So I was getting into that stuff by reading it in the wrong accent and really digging it. Then I worked back thru some of the very careful metricians of modern times, like Zukofsky, or Stephen Jonas, or Williams, or some of Olson, some of Kelly, back to the Elizabethan stuff, which is very very lovely. I can definitely get off on Romantic Poetry because I see it as the beginning of our own history, of that transposition of religious consciousness, with Blake and Wordsworth and Coleridge, when poets become conscious of the metaphysical function in the acting of writing poetry itself. The Seventeenth Century Metaphysical poets (with the exception of one American, Edward Taylor, who wrote poems and then wrote his sermons as analyses of the poems) are not writing poems as a spiritual activity. They're not solving their problems of dealing with God in their poems.

There's an awful lot to be learned from lending an ear to the best practitioners. And doing that, and having to confront the exquisite attention that English prosodists have given to their own sounds creates a kind of standard, and my poetry in the last two or three years has become much more attentive to the specific sound syllable to syllable; not that I'm writing anything like formal English verse, but that density of attention.

In *A Special View of History*, Olson makes a very sweeping statement about the nature of the cosmology of the Western World being fixed by the Babylonians and the Hittites in the image of a duality of chaos and order. The creation of value, since then, has had to do with the imposition of a pattern on a chaotic material; and since Whitehead say, with the new cosmology, that picture of things has come to an end; there is a seeing that processes of order emerge from the natural, emerge *in* the natural, and are not imposed upon it. So that, say, the image of a flower rising out of the mud does not involve the imposition of a paradigm of order upon a chaos but the realization of potentials within

11

the given ground substance to begin with. I think that that holds as a description of the total body of Olson's work, as opposed to X or Y or Z's work which might be understood as the imposition of order on chaotic experience. Olson's public work may represent the jewels or the flowers, the most realized forms of a constant activity, which is going on on all levels at all times. The Olson collection itself [in the Library at Storrs] is the matrix or the ground out of which those flowers arise. There's one box of papers he put together sometime before he died of all the notes had had from 1959, 1960, 1961, the period really between the two volumes of *Maximus*, where he took it and put it all in order and dated it. It represents a kind of intermediary world between simply publishable material and any number of scattered thousands of pieces of paper which are not. If you look in any one of those two thousand envelopes, you don't find that any one envelope represents any particular specific period of time. So basically what I'm doing for my thesis is studying those papers, cataloguing them, relating them to the finished work that comes out of them (or the variations in the different materials that emerge in the finished work), and locating the material in his own library that he's reading and incorporating at the same time."

This book attempts to bring together the different threads of Stein's work: the poetry, the meditation (in the "cumulus" material and other specific poems), the music (in the "Buzz Saws"), the drawing, the photography, and the cosmology (in this preface). The cosmology, however, is dynamically involved with the synthesis of these modes into one creative and cetripetal activity. Stein is not simply a jack of many trades; he is a master of the continuous transformation of one form of energy and activity into another. There is no outside model for the entire internal process (as geography for Olson); thus the specific skills, images, and practices can occur in a variety of dimensions; they are all brought back into the body, as voice, as rhythm, as lotus, as motor coordination, as neural map, and the body of the poet becomes literally the body of the whole work. The very process of moving from activity to activity allows the activities to shed light on each other and reveal aspects of each other thru the differences between them. Any one activity is an overview on any other activity, even as it is its antagonist in the doing (one cannot articulate and non-articulate at the same time). The changes in the body and the personal individuation of one who is working on such a dynamic are recorded collectively in the differential developments of each process, almost as a metaphor for the uniquely-endowed organs and systems of the body. Stein explains his work thusly:

"I think that I take each particular thing, say drawing, music, building a cumulus, writing poems, meditating, as if it were, at the time, the dominant part of my work. So that, in a sense, each one has a representation of all the others as if each were subordinate to each in any particular context of making. While I'm building a cumulus the first thing that's in my attention is building a cumulus. At the same time what it accumulates is precisely the same energies that are received in meditation. Then a poem comes at the point when I'm dissolving the cumulus and it appears as though the cumulus is the source of the poem, as if I built the cumulus in order to write a poem about it.

12

And I think that meditation and poetry work in a similar way. The kinds of concerns I get into from writing will appear in another form during meditation. At that moment it's as if the poetry had to do with my life and meditation had to do with a different kind of work that includes everything else, that any given poem might have meditation simply as its subject matter; where I am writing from the same intentionality that is directing meditation, the material will be permitted to have its verbal form in a poem. Meditation and poetry would be the polarity: one a direction toward an inarticulate moment of thought that precedes language, and the poem the opposite intention, letting the material take its full articulation (be fully articulated).

It never seemed possible for me to research Yonkers. Yet clearly the paradigm that Olson was presenting was that the great cosmological change in the Twentieth Century was that what was spirit was now matter and what was matter was now spirit, that the old dichotomy between a spiritual and a material was dead, and that anything of a higher order had to be discovered thru the specific, thru the concrete, and now thru the general, thru the universal, or thru the abstract. In his case that meant thru the body, thru one's physical movements, to the actual territory that one occupied, and the concrete history of the places that he occupied, and thru that, from that specificity, to the specificity of the Earth and the Universe. I never felt that I had such a subject given to me. I didn't feel as though I could arbitrarily select some spot and go study it; that seemed literally arbitrary to me. I wasn't interested in Yonkers, and I didn't have any particular sort of feel for history that he had had long before he came even to those senses of things. But as I got more and more into meditation I began more and more to think of it as a similar kind of process. The unearthing of my own consciousness, the settling of the psyche into the body, etc., represented at the same time for me the meditation that for him, later, was the meditation on the place. What I have lately evolved in dream writing is a kind of reworking of this geographical question. The dreams seem to be setting out an imaginary geography; that is, they take place in places with names, New Hampshire, the North Pole, several places on the Bronx River, several places in Manhattan, Brooklyn, etc., and in some way it may turn out that I will have to settle that imaginary geography back into their actual localities in the same way that I have to settle psyche into my body. But I have to begin by getting my body and the inside world in order before I can be in a house or live in a place.

What happens in meditation is that there are any number of different models for what I am doing that occur to me at different times depending on how my mind is spinning at that time. There are any number of different doors, and each is a possible beginning point. Actually I got this idea from Lama Govinda's *Psychological Attitudes in Buddhist Thought*. In early Buddhism meditation seems to be directed on space itself, space not as in an abstract mathematical space, but existential space, that is, space which has a center insofar as there are things that are near to you and things that are far to you, and that things are happening inside of you; objects in your ken are nearer or further away, and influence you or have an impact on you totally on the basis of their distance. You experience space in those terms, that your self is just the foreground, and all the things happening in your mind, happening in

13

your body, happening in your emotional body, happening inside you, are
absolutely continuous with what's outside. But the importance of the
events decreases with the square of their distances from you, as a
force of gravity or light radiating from a center. What interests me
very constantly (and this has been with me since the time of writing
those "Tarot Journals" [*Io/4*, enlarged edition, 1973, originally pub-
lished in *Aion*, 1964] years ago) is the very clear experience of when a
thought reaches the level of being an actual phrase or a sentence in
your mind. That it has already formulated itself previously. So that
what you're getting is a kind of extension of it into verbal form. One
exercise which I'm constantly doing is attempting to be aware of the
earliest moment in which a thought begins to arise and hold my attention
on that place, impeding its articulation into verbal form in order to
stay as close as possible to what's happening absolutely right now on a
mental level, the poem being the extreme opposite of that, where you
force things to articulation, where you force every mental intuition to
its articulation. The difference between an utterance that would occur
in a poem and any other utterance would literally have to be, that in
a poem there is some sensitivity to the process of utterance itself.
The actual temporal flow of the poem has a sense of depth to it, i.e.,
that in the end the inarticulate kernel of any given utterance should be
felt as present in the actual utterance, but not by articulation.

The emotional content comes thru too because it's the emotional
content that's going to be directing the actual flow of the poem. A
similar thing happens in meditation in relation to emotion, that nor-
mally you are not aware of emotional qualities as a continuing ongoing
flowing process; only at heightened moments are you aware of something
that you would call emotion; nonetheless there is an emotional body
that's in activity all the time. Then another process of meditation
is staying with the actual flow of very subtle emotional states. What
I mean by "an emotion" is: a feeling of excitement, of affection, of
anger. When anything that you would call "emotions" is discovered by
you as taking place in your body, watch it, staying absolutely with its
flow as it develops. In a poem a similar thing is happening in that you
permit the emotional flow to be directing the contour of the language
and the physical aspect of the language.

I have a sense of all these things developing in me together. And
I began getting interested in meditating and writing at the same time.
It's been posed to me that there must be some conflict between the two,
since meditation is ostensibly an inarticulate absolutely private ex-
perience with its "goal" in the thing itself, without any external re-
sult being from it, an activity purposely directed toward nonarticula-
tion. But also there is the sense that meditation tends to be associa-
ted with some sort of salvationist mystique, that you meditate in order
to do something with your person, to save your soul, or destroy your ego
in order to save your ego. Then the poets doing the poetry that most
concerns me consistently put forth that the actual spiritual activity of
the writing itself should be the sufficient spiritual activity, as if to
be involved in some extra-writing spiritual activity somehow were a de-
valuing of writing itself (not to take one's position fully in language).
At the same time, at any point when I'm involved with people who are
solely into meditation, the engagement with writing seems like an ego

trip. It's a dilemma that sometimes appears to me as a conflict, but only insofar as other people have posed it to me as such and I've identified with them and so become fearful that it was so. I don't ultimately feel that it is. They're both total activities, and if your sense of totality, of wholeness, is something which relates to every moment in itself, and that every moment is a whole in itself, there would seem to be the possibility of having what would seem to be competing hierarchies of experience which are not competing except insofar as that at any one moment one activity may have a lower position. Poetry is secondary to meditation, or meditation is secondary to poetry, only depending on the moment that is engaged in the activity. In a certain sense they both have to do with processes of keying up attention to time itself. In some sense the ultimate object of all meditation practice is the most concrete sense of the flow of time, as is the most concrete object of attention in writing.

The material I pick up thru reading comes back around in other ways, in all the different spheres of things. When I was building the cumulus, reading the *Ogotemmeli* conversations were very important to me because there was a particular image world being presented there as a primary metaphor for everything, particularly in the image of the grainery and the image of the anthill, running them thru cosmology, social organization, categories of plants, animals, etc. [Marcel Griaule: *Conversations with Ogotemmeli: An Introduction to Dogon Religious Ideas*]. On the one level there was simply the coincidence of there being such a cosmology and my reading it at that time, such that building the cumulus involved me in making my own visualization of a cosmology structure; on the other hand there was a particular feeling about the images that were presented there that was directly translated into the things I was putting into the cumulus. As I was building it, I had the sense that what I was doing was building an image of my body; an internal image of my body was building up very slowly, as if in the possibility of an internal consciousness, and I was building an image of *it*. Much of what I was reading then, not just *Ogotemmeli* but Santillana [Giorgio de Santillana and Hertha von Dechend: *Hamlet's Mill: An Essay on Myth & the Frame of Time*] or things in various cosmological systems, was making me aware of parallel processes. At the same time I was building up a kind of language so that I could speak from energies that were coming in meditation without having to talk about my body or specifically what was happening to me. The difficulty of talking about internal perceptions is that there is no language for them, and insofar as there *is* a language, it's extremely clinical and very far removed from the actual experiences themselves. Building the cumulus provides then a series of images which can be used without even talking about the body but which make available for writing the energies which meditation is providing. So, take for example a poem, in this case the Cumulus poem in particular. In the one sense it *is* a meditation and its structure is in some sense *like* a meditation. It's not *about* meditation, but it is about certain Buddhist concerns, like a principle in things (or in Universe) to create duration; nonetheless the underlying play of energies in the poem becomes available by having made the cumulus as an image; it's almost like a feeling in my abdomen, crudely as that, a feeling of solidity in my abdomen, a warm radiation of energy, which was also somehow built into the cumulus. Certain people coming and seeing it could feel certain vibes about it, and

15

my sense was that I was building an objective correlative for those inner states, from which I made the poem as another correlative, in writing down the images from it. It's like when you dream something and then you write down the dream, and writing the dream is in a sense a redreaming in that the energies are really reactivated and given a different structure. Similarly, the specific relationship between reading a text and then writing something from reading it is very much like having a dream and then writing the dream. You only get one chance. You can't go back later and read it a second time and try to reproduce the conditions in which you can use those images. There is also a discontinuity between where the text comes to you as the solidification or identification and verbalization of some initiatory process and where the text is initiatory itself, not in the sense that it gives you the experience but that it provides that the attitude struck in you in the process of reading becomes something which you yearn to possess more fully. So that having read Trungpa's book, having read *Lilith*, having read *Ogotemmeli*, having read Olson, provides imaginations of kinds of worlds which it then becomes your business to realize. But the text is not in any sense a replacement for that process of building one.

Over the years I've read and reread pictures of the history of modern physics, and they interest me not so much because they are pictures of physical reality which I can believe but because they are the activity of a mind on our scale dealing with the limits in size, either the very small or the very large, and they produce particular sorts of mental structures which can only come about by the engagement of a mind on our scale with things at those limits. Whereas I am very skeptical, as pretentious as that sounds, of the ultimate meaning of the knowledge of physical reality on the basis of elementary particle physics, nevertheless it provides instances where it becomes necessary to create modes of thought which become extremely useful in dealing with other areas where we exist in a similar relationship in terms of scale. For instance, in meditation, in following any process, whether mental, physical, or emotional, for any duration whatsoever, even if it's for a fraction of a second, one is engaged in a microreality, and the questions of calculus, whether they're infinitesimals or not infinitesimals, and how reality is altered when you're dealing on microlevels becomes a very immediate question, and the reading of simplified popularized elementary particle literature is a kind of magnetizing of the attention to the microscopic which provides aids, clues, for focusing it in terms of actual experience. I find, for instance, there's a constant experience of light waves, of waves of light illuminating from the eyes and from the whole body in meditation. At first the waves start by your being aware of the sizzling light of retinal activity; if you keep your attention on that there begin to be visible wave flows. As you experience the contours of that, you become involved in smaller and smaller intervals. I read in Koestler's *Roots of Coincidence* that the amount of energy necessary to stimulate a retinal flash, a perceptible retinal flash, is incredibly small, something like five quanta whatever that means. Whatever it means it means that we have actual experience that the fabric of normal experience is continuously remade of events which are, anyway, on a submolecular level. The rapidity with which the formation of an intention, of a thought which in one moment is going to bind the con-

16

tours of the next ten seconds or two seconds or fraction of a second directly related to the mathematical structures which physicists have evolved to talk about elementary particles and which are required on the most elementary level of what would seem to be psychology. In order to have a scientific psychology you would have to start off with some-thing as mathematically fine as the many-dimensional world of particle physics. Koestler talks of a certain aspect of particle speculation in which the physicists have invented something they call virtual spaces; the virtual space is at any given moment the projection of the probability of what's going to happen to the particle at x moment in the future. And this is going to be different for the particle every moment because every moment contains an identifiable measurable formula for what are called compresent dispositional factors, which are in no sense physically present in the event but are representable in some probability relation of what's going to happen to it. So that what you have at any given moment of time is a picture of all time. At moment N you have not only the events at N but the probability for what's going to happen in that space for any moment in the future; at N + 1 that probability is going to be absolutely revised in terms of what actual event does take place. And that model seems to have a lot to do with all the questions of determinism, free will, and how we measure consciousness as we move in our own time-space. Emotional reality is always forward-leaning. What you feel in an emotion is directional as it begins to flow. Simi-larly, any thought from that, any actual intellectual activity, treats that as if it were the past and throws out an image binding the future, as if to impose on the flow of real time a construction which has a specific formation at a given moment in virtual time. And I think that one of my concerns in both meditation and in poetry is to let the actual flow of real time play against the projection of virtual time. In other words, at any given moment any given line will have within it the potent-iality for the development of the poem, which will then become further specified in the next line. It's not that I'm throwing down a pattern over time but, more complexly, letting any pattern that's thrown down at any given moment play against the actual flow of time, so that any pat-tern at any given moment plays against the actual flow of time and is capable of changing and moving in any number of different directions."

Stein's cosmology is really a rotating set of dialectics and possi-bilities which are pulled into and out of the conscious field. An inter-view done at a particular time captures an angle of the whole, plus his immediate excitement and engagement with what he is presently involved in as an idea. The discussion which produced this preface reveals Stein's interests and concerns only insofar as they are focused in the energies and attentions of the moment. He is rarely retrospective. Other discussions, not recorded, have dealt with the sound of the blood flowing thru the brain and the electricity of the mind, the relation between the gravitational field of a star and the gravitational pull of the mind (such that mind and star are the *only* literal metaphors for each other), the Stonehenge-Atlantis-Rosicrucian connections, and the relation of Olson's geographical space to astronomical-astrological time-space, etc. etc. Thus, this preface should be viewed as a single temporally-idosyncratic statement of his work, which is changed by the

17

conditions and circumstances of the next moment, even contradicted in
parts by them, as the thought process continues to rotate. The pre-
face is to serve as an introduction to Stein's work and an objective
response by the author to some of the patterns this book brings into
being and is brought into being by. The following statements come from
our discussion, and are included at the end because they are not really
directly in any of the previous flows whose premises they extend.

"I like the Don Juan thing in Book Three, in *Ixtlan* [*Journey to
Ixtlan* by Carlos Castaneda]: that one's business is not being trapped
by ordinary reality or surreal reality. It's sort of like the Tantric
Buddhist position; what one has to learn is the powers of the mind to
create entities, and to be aware that the realities that are engaged in
are not simply phenomenological realities. Once you become engaged in
the creating of imagination you have in some way an effect on something
that's beyond yourself. The entities conjured in the drawings are tan-
tric exercises in visualizing horrible things. If I sit and meditate
and look at anything that has any kind of complex structure I start
having practically acid hallucinations; I start seeing all kinds of dif-
ferent faces, and that in itself is an extremely interesting thing, the
question of what the link is between the imagined image and the physical
reality of the imagined image. For instance, Goethe's color theory,
and the exercises in which you stimulate your retina in different ways.
It's subjective, and at the same time it has known physiological cor-
relates, so it's the one place where the duality of subjective and ob-
jective doesn't exist. If you stay tuned to the retinal activity, eith-
er with eyes closed or open eyes, so that you're stimulating internally
the activity of the retina, so that you're seeing lights, what really
starts happening is that it becomes very very easy to project an image
into that. All you have to do is start thinking of rose wheels or
mandala patterns or Mayan hieroglyphs or Egyptian hieroglyphs or any
other multiform image that you have stored in your imagination and it
will automatically be physically realized on the **grid** of the retinal
activity, and that process is a ground for recircling in a certain
sense the relationship between mental activity and physical realization.
The drawing has to do with that; you're involved in some hand process,
hand and eye working together, the middle voice of hand and eye where
you're being both active and perceptive at the same time to the realiz-
ation of an image which will have psychic relevance.

One is not only, by becoming engaged with powerful images, dis-
covering them all over the place, but is in some sense actually con-
juring them in the field of events themselves. You have no way of
knowing whether they're using you or you're using them. The most sim-
ple phenomena, which seem perfectly ordinary in the Newtonian frame or
in the frame of ordinary reality, are absolutely startling, and I don't
see that the problem is less so whichever is true, whether there's an
anima mundi with a telepathic net that we're all involved in or whether
it's simply that we're all involved in an onwardly moving temporal re-
ality."

18

TEN   TUNES

The Danger

for all
your life
          not
to have comfortable
furniture

I noticed

my nose

taking its shape

after yours

OLD CHAIR, HELLO!
OLD CHAIR, HELLO!

I am low
I am low

You are large
You are large

I rise out of sleep
Old chair
            you are there
            you are there

Protect me from
The crack in the door

the ancestors
slide down the bow of heaven
after long
long rain
for many days
the fogs were low
over silent Irish green lawns October
love and coffee odors, music of harps

one held the hammer in his green green
hand and
lost his self in a closet

He is looking at something
he must do with his right hand.

He doesn't know much about
the top of his headpiece.

He doesn't know very much.

He knows what he looks at
looks back at him.

One day he was watching
the stones in his room
and the stones began to undulate and quicken.

That that was not the first time that had happened
he remembered.

For often the thought of solid things
had seemed not solid to him.

That was ok.

Now they were disposed on the bench
and he was adamant to toy with the wrenches.

The bolts were tight
but only bolts they were.

That's why I say
he didn't know much about his headpiece.

It looked like some kind of cheap sombrero
with a bent rim.

You could stop the sun with it.

There are
among men
certain masters.

Do not seek
to find out who
they are.

The moon is over the river.

Enormous hawks
disturb the question anyway. The wind
from their wings
is enough to knock over your car.
You do not know
what you ride in.

Gold are its posts.

Blue is the cloth of its canopy
covered with stars.

The day of the bell

at the bottom
of motion
when the water
stops
and the deva
is a frog
possessed upon his lotus pod

*

walking on a bridge above the swamp
I came to a joint in the way
arched by a gate of flame
and did take council how to be beyond it

I sat
at the ledge
            and lo
half my body was shot away

the smoke from the gate went
up above the gum trees
and from the azure
into which it rose
a goddess rode
in lotus rest

holding my legs in a delicate basket

and lo
her face
was shot away
and I held a book
of images of it
painted on ivory cards

*

though love is not commerce
she sang

if you will come
to where I am not
and make of me an image
for which I may care not
and burn it in the flame that burns between us
and by which we are one

this dream
          will open
and prove a true one

misty morning
pan pipes

hairy fingers ripple the stops
fluted airs of the goldcrouched goatgod
horny moon airs
music of the silver gaze
music of the lake

he says the day is grey
but for my tune off it
up among the pine tall rods

I have an egg
I hatch in my crotch

its shell is the color of heaven

              snow patch on
glazed dawn lake

pool still

when mind
is like a pool
the mud will rise

cold prose

when body is not
discontinuous
its spaces

  . . .

red barn farm
one
     willow rise

car ride
   astride

    pressure of land
   in form of over-
hanging cliff-jaggs

  . . .

the contemplation of one's spaces
reverses the nature of desire

  . . .

I take place
out there

  . . .

sun through
    snow mist
late march north
green mountain
  morning storm

cars
    can't pass

measure risk skillfully

giant weighted
trailer truck
impending

on the rear of farrari

. . .

my model
is of
unfolding
        not
development

            all
the parts
of the work
implied in the come

                    who?
is independent mind

neither hope nor fear
to trouble the bowelry

. . .

I want

. . .

snow mist
   just
        ahead

you must
see the situation
with *skillful means*

use space
as though it were
the only instrumentality
of wisdom
           vis:

     any vehicle
     ahead of you

     casts a cloud of mist and snow
     behind

     That as you are
     constrained to follow

     so your way is blind

HERMES' NIGHT SONG

what is the name of your god if not
Harpocrates?

                thieves
come to this place from
all the world

sell yourself or
buy me
        or
give me the goods or
here are   the goods

moon over harbor

long
    night
of waiting for the
whole sky
to pass it by

Harpocrates

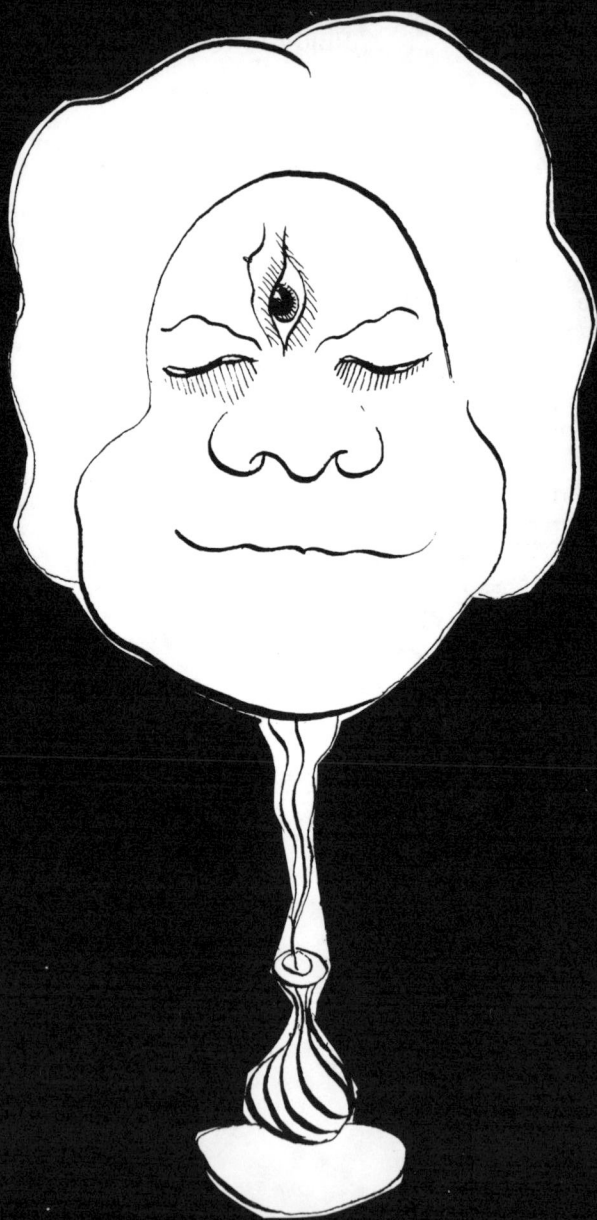

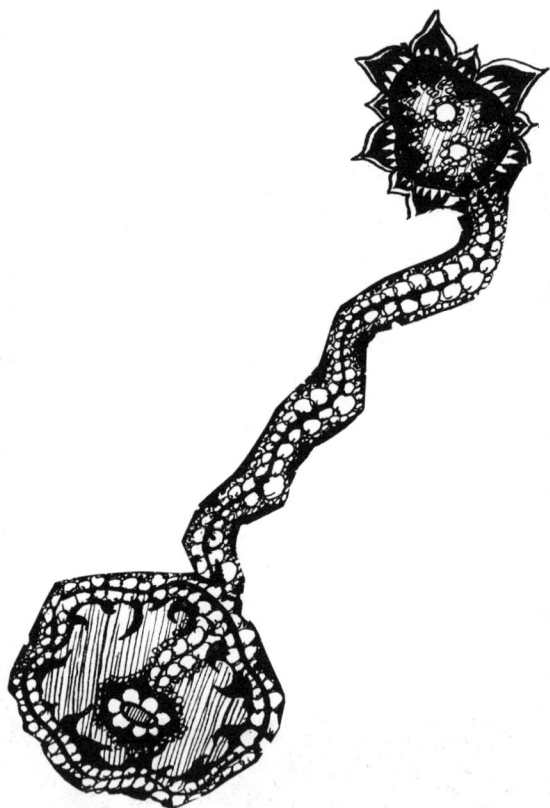

SPACES

SPACES

1

it is white

*

the argument
from domiciles

*

I found the ultimate metaphor for mind

*

a door

*

they sing in harmony

*

and nail

*

the lovers to the song

*

the carriage passes

*

the openness of space was like its fountain

I am doing the right thing

*

give the water back to the water

*

it makes no sense

*

as he steps off the boat
he takes
only what he needs along
with him

*

every morning

*

to talk about something

*

I am doing the right thing

*

it makes no sense

*

this expresses respect for the water

*

I went to Yosemite National Park
and I saw some huge
water fall

a dream

*

not mind

*

the parsley leaves
yellow
        wither
at the outside
green
        grow
up at
the stem

*

words
        the
riverrun with
in for
a source of them

*

mind

*

stand
like a stupid man
                become
that statue
            let
water run new
rushing spring

*

the sound
outside

the hands
within

the lock works

4

an egg
in his hands

the color of heaven

*

I am the lawn

*

if a bird then
a bath for him

*

the colors

a nest for him

*

he is born

*

soon he
takes the moments
of our lives to
mark his passages

though only
such moments
as to him
belong

*

the next day
he flies away
with us
against the storm

*

to get there

make a wedge for him

*

    come
back again o
           bird-to-the-east

*

nest work

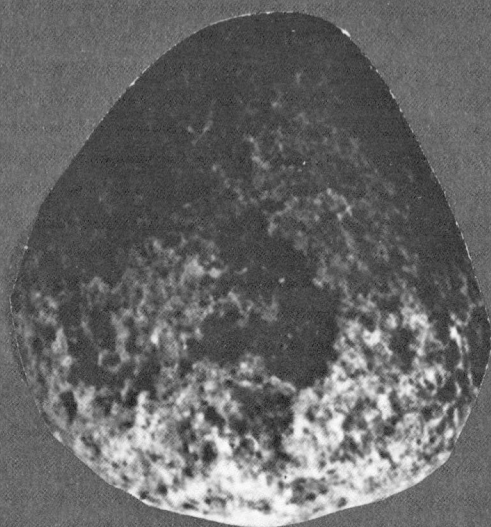

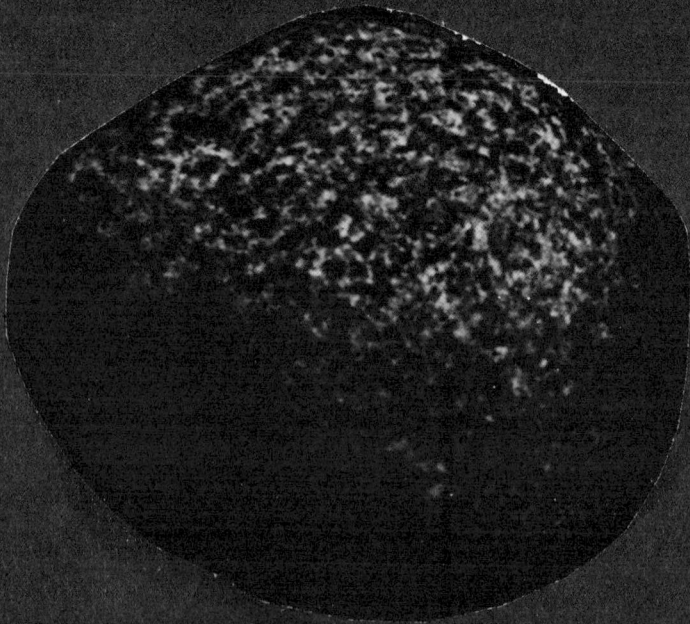

BUZZ SAWS

BUZZ   SAWS

1

it   is
over night that
her   privately done up so
a square dude like you'd know how
it   how it swamps one   I'd
like it not
so fast so
as I could   lean on some
sense I had of what I had
'twas done to her   never
predict the future
rang the gong

in the corner
of the room her
listening range   the cat
behind the leg

how to
take the
kill

everything

without (its

telling

roses
in the dawn

the new pool still not watered

how to tell everyone
how to tell everyone

```
   as
it is your task it
is a basket
and mine among
the branches
            hammocklike in May


                              a movie
I saw
in my childhood


depicting myself
in a prior
condition
of childhood


I was a still child, dispossessing
myself of
all things.


Was
Is.
```

4

the the the

of

stepping aside from his his

shutting up and giving up   room

standing back in the wings and not not flying

standing there is is
is already is having
getting gotten there

getting there

where would you
would you go
                go
back again
              again
                  go
back again

OUT OUT

leisure
of old was
as false as
leisure
now   who

could begin to
rest as
though there
might be
a park where
one might go

WARNING:

when the time
comes
        how
will we know
who you are?

Andy had
a book
full of coin they
date back
years I
couldn't really get it what it
was
    why
he kept
copper
pennies
in that book
when I was a boy
Andy
knew astronomy
he learned from Kagan's paper back Andy knew
the planet
name
rhyme

it was not
different
from now
        how
to break
routine
I would go
to *his* house
and we'd commence
                   an
idol he
had
kept
    in his cabinet
we did not name
flames
were lit to him words
made
    to make him
move us
        music
was part of it

I had risen
before I started
not to show I
had risen. It
was father
poking his head
in the door.
                He
put on that he was
                just
                    aimlessly wandering

But as it happened
he needed to take out
articles from the drawer
                        yet
next
I asked
was it   he was now to go down town to
his office I
might find cause in it
that early
to arise, but he said no, he
was looking for his golf gloves.

11

all that
she had to say was
not to let my
hair go
down the drain as
yester-
day
there was flooding
badly downstairs
and much of what had been my "papers" stored there
were
now
no more

I heard her heart say karma, I was cause
I who belonged to an alien sociology...

golden
towels
on the towel rack

today it's
pt pt pt pt
          chk chk wuuuuuushshshshsss
ssssssstops and
goes
     today
she is at
her desk at
twenty to seven
while he
lies
supinenineninenine
a vollume
of the Brittanica
in his hand

I gottagettagoing
UP UP

sit UP
set UP

pt pt pt pt
chk chk chk chk

wshshshsh

```
      /
p p p /
    /   k t p
p p p /
    /   k tttttt
p p p /
        k t t


put up    the cat
                  trick it it
sits it
has its
spot
      p t p p t p as

  <       >
I I I I   I
sit     not
that
stopt
      as the
cat but

Pt Pt Pt Pt Pt Pt Pt Pt it
                            <       >
                            I I I I   I
SIT!   SIT!
```

I know in
art it's
what fills
the rest when
one part goes
awry

moment to moment

it seems good advice to
seek out how
for every irritation
attention
is the
        means to be
applied

birds
occupy
the budding
trees
to the north and west
the sky last
night
was dry
but rain
prevents
the repetition
I had hoped
to sit zazen
under the
same tree where
I sat then

15

april
twenty one
can

words once
put get
gone gone come
again ? get
gone again

I
love
to be in
charge, of, things, if
they
make
me their prince I am
splendid
        glad

are they
my
words then they
spring from
my words

is every
one
the king

you can go to
the country not
think it
at all
for a year or two it
doesn't
get a
way from you that that that that that that that that

                                                     stand

up
now
hit
one more blow who
knows anything
of national
politics

now

*

we do.
and we do.
you do. But he
for chrissake don't and she don't and we
better gettagoddam better goddam. But
they don't.

*

  and what
did you
pick up on?

            this
is what there is
to be begun

metal over this
part
    flat
slabs of canvas
to blot out That

the dog
twists at
his own
tail the cat
bites
against morning

I sit straight up to hear what
has this to do
do with ending, curing until
all
beings
until all
will

*

guidelines

guidelines

hear me   say   no
killing it
is not   what   it
seems   to be   the
mat
makes
a means of
death but but this
is by by no means

*

I don't
find on
this
issue
there is an
other
side

side

side

side

side

ENTITIES

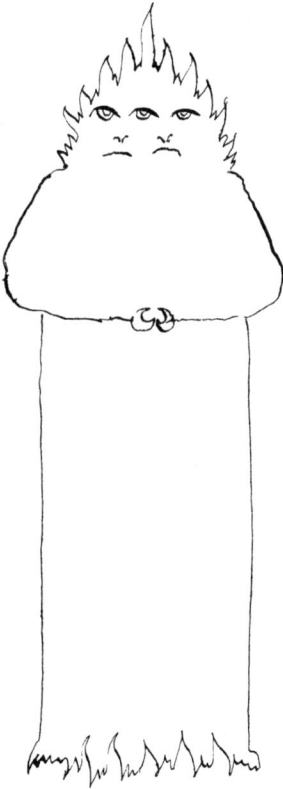

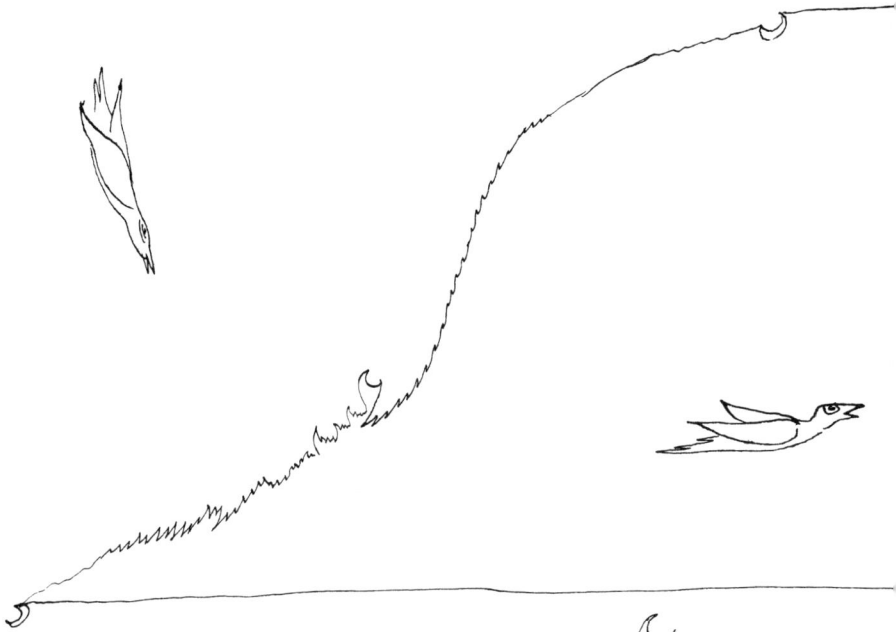

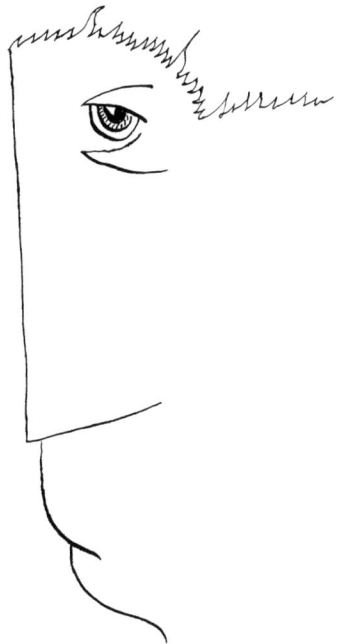

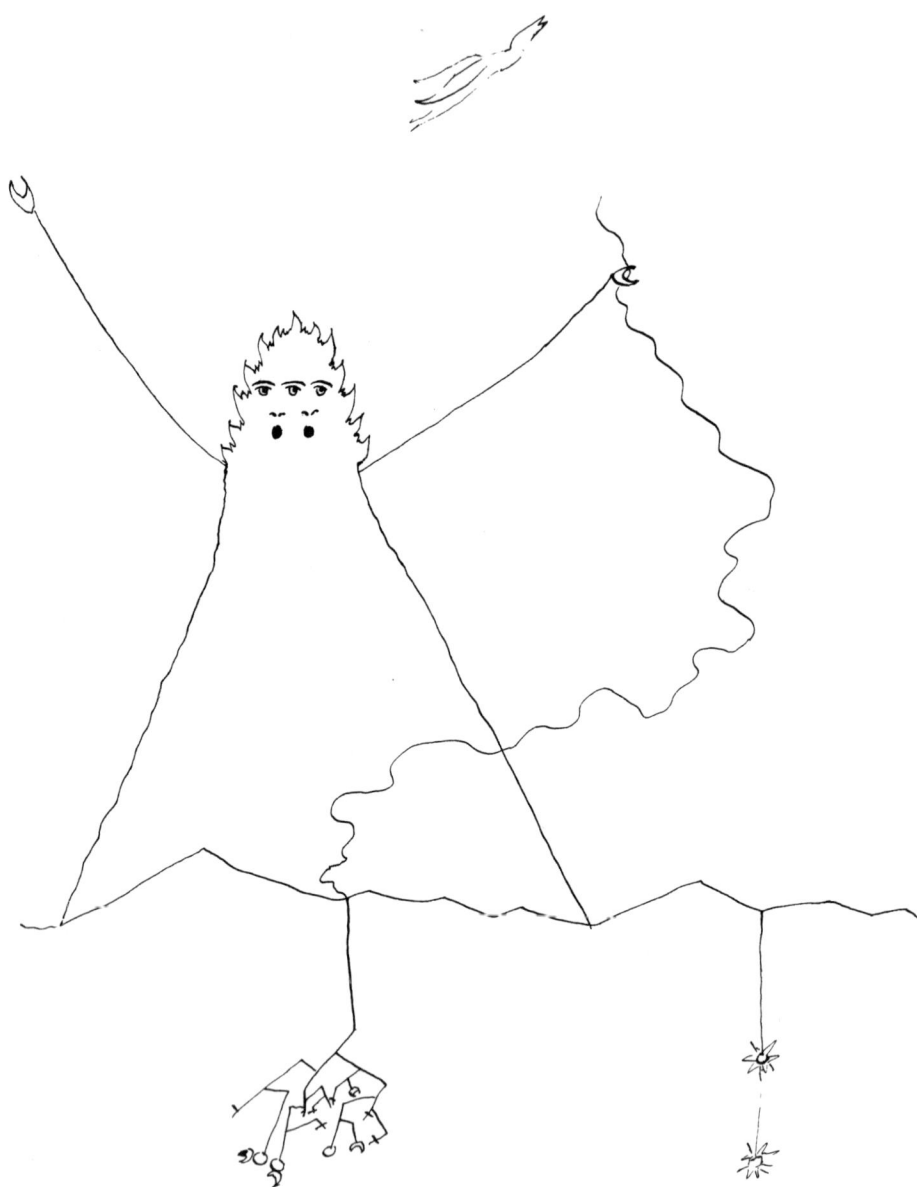

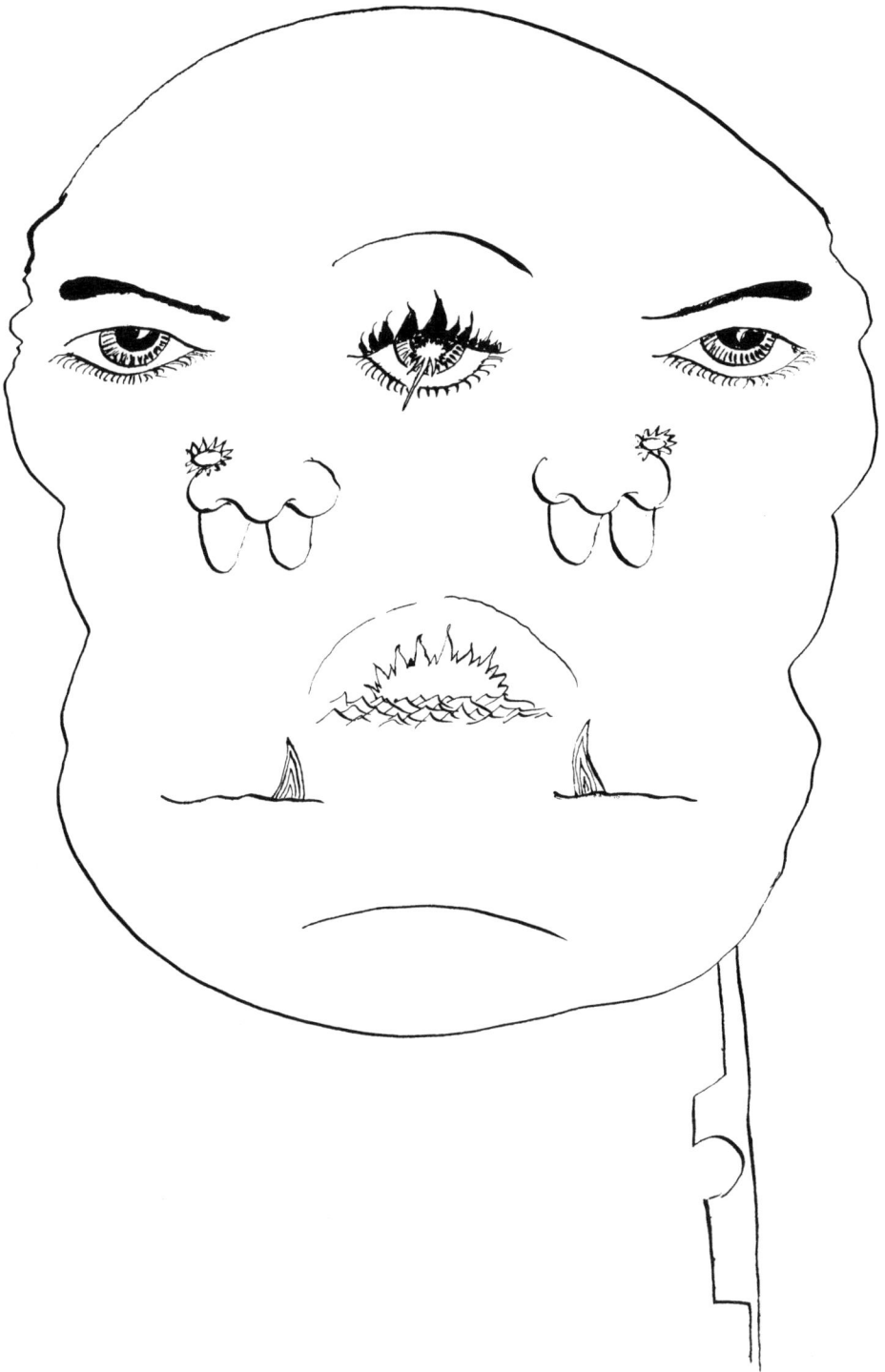

3 DOCTRINAL POEMS

Two ways
always
to think about
the organs:

Wonder at how they
hold together

Panic at how they
surely
come apart.

Of earth
likewise
no otherwise
than to be here
briefly

what if you're a flower
among construction projects
                              do you
re-order
what order
you think you've
got
    to dodge the asphalt
                           or

I'm no flower
                some
master cactus
                some small
aloe

There is no decay
of body
        only
life-activity
resumed on lesser
scale

(wakeful ego talking

but I am
 prior
  even to
my ignorance
           (no comfort

the body
  will live
as long as it can
                then

ancient relapse

       *

rain later
run down
outside

I must exhaust myself

as if I were all outside

a man can push so hard
and must
until there is no more
need of doing this

what is your goal
she said

proverbial:

to unpeal
skin after skin
until a blossom
until it burn itself

when will a woman

       *

sit
sit
husk
you lose control
form is rigid
motion
love is sex
thought in time
transgress the social
make it new on
all planes
that means
suit yourself

out

there is a small
change
nothing really
noticeable
leg pains
turn out to be bearable
the discipline
is not what it was
believed
to be
before

the mess of social life
the missed significance
or holding off from it
you are as mad as you look

I'm ok
        except with people

when
      at last
I had said in myself yes
I will begin
love starts slow
under summer
railway bridge

but that's where you <u>live</u>
she said

the discipline

was not to be believed

nothing turns out

I was not too slow

        *

        and then
to give it over
                this
has always
been my
thought of it
to get it on
and done
        then

even now I keep up the practice of watching it
fall away

            have
no possession
of her
attributes her
skinny walk down
the road
make yourself
on your own time
momentary
completion
is all I
think to
come to
home
is not so
mutually
derived

        *

Our Lady's Way

The Girdle of the Sky

The wisdom
will
be saved
      that
is assured
      or
what
 of it
    was
wisdom
    will not
need
   salvation

it happens again
new
or it is not
wisdom

after the fact

what will be re-
membered
is not now
to be
discerned
now
to continue
a process
already long
begun:

resistance.

       Not
but
as the mind
tends
its advantage

```
                turn
with it
the slow stars
                yet
are not
dislodged
from infallible mansion

we have not
found out

the bear
is as far
to the north
as none but a
bear
could be
        the three
Housatonic
hunters
chase him
```

pile of coins
for blood

who lives who
dies
    goes
over
    stays
back in home
ground

    luxury
he calls it
our wish to secure
homeground

an animal
as if whose hands
ever secure a
future for it

a vegetable mass
at a sea floor
making from the sea its
self by such
selection

to watch
    not
what the mind knows
but the act of seizure
by such hands for it

*

there is no
social
history
of it
    only
the possibility
time affords

the work of a few men un-
known to each other
lifting the mountain

with the majestic
certainty
of an elephant's walk
wherever he
does find himself

the fragile
leafage
parted

                    2

outside
     all
   things
        are
contemporaneous
        the meaning of my life, this
     first
          must
     be blown apart
                    reduced
     to elemental
   time and fire
               so close
          a watch
               kept
                    that
     no story of it be
   believed
               if formed
               to think
     is but to move an anxious hand

flood rains

*

stopt reach

*

after many centuries a
look about the
foreground

*

I write myself not
out of some
self-adulation but
because I
occupy the
foreground

*

spring into shimmering trees

*

or any space there is, it
spreads
        thence

*

and when I seem
to denegrate the intellect

*

Diana's pool
swelling rocky banks

*

the divers from the tops of stones and trees
risking the autumn shallows

I tear at the intervals

the narrowing furrows

4

the damage
done
is not
the measure

the river
floods
the ponds
swamp the grasses

*

wake up, drugged
spirit, matter
and time
in which you lodge

watch what
forces
are given you for
deflection

delicate
white
parts

*

```
        where
does the root
begin

        is
this a burgeoning



I have only to tell what
my body learns
                its
liquid colors
            underparts
                        of thought
                                    let
thought
begin


white light
to meet
red heat:


the play of womanly energy's endless instructing
```

THE CUMULUS

THE CUMULUS

1

rock   seed

a frog on the left bole

a fish in the cord

a bird on the little white beach stones

These stones I found on
Long Island.
Other stones, I found in Monterey
on the beach
last January.

Robert Alpert
and James Polachek
and myself
were walking there.

And a postcard
on a gift box
of an ornamental bird.

I pick it up.

It boasts a golden belly and a gold throat.

Lulla Adler gave me the box.

Its cover is inlaid mandala mother of pearl.

Another box is hidden among the coinage
covered with scatter of parsley leaves.

Smaller. Green. A personal
patch of gaberdine
has been inside it now for more than a decade.

Elk horns are on the milk stool.
And a double globe of crystal
is next to the elk horns.
And next to the milk stool
I have built a kind of altar.

If it seems I have little to do but move ideas:

a problematic of being there.

Behind but wider than
the nest of things
I hatch inside my room.

And inward of but yet not wider than

Eye-buzz.

And with me
and more solid still
the making process that ends in solid things.

    High trees
at the foot of the city.

Arbitrarily scattered cotyledons.

An azure stone upon the hat-pin altar piece
a present from Bialy.

Clear. Mystery. Pleasure. Celestial. Solid. Small.

All

there is.

All is all there is.

From the mouth of the frog
on the left bole

from the spill of the basket-horn all

evidence of plenty.

Each of the many stones as
All there is.

The wheel of the sun
on the part of the loom.

The wooden blocks
are All there is.

The little plastic vessels
All there is.

The seed
was planted
almost
now
two years ago.

I was living in the pink house.

No. The seed was planted
years before that, even.

When I was living in the pink house
on a rainy day in what must have been October
in Gloucester, or Lanesville, Cape Ann,
thinking of my part of the pink house at Storrs

I knew about the terminal moraine

and wanted to possess in my house
such a stone as I had seen
spilled in all possible variety of sizes
often at Pigeon Cove.

Georger Butterick suggested the term Cumulus for it.

And that was when we were reading at Trinity
and I read a group of my poems
entitled
Buzz Saws.

That stone you could call the seed

but that's not right because
the space in which the cumulus has gathered
had other precedent

and also the thinking and grounding
that founded the stone

began with a poem Jonathan Greene showed me many
years ago.

It was part, I think, of something Paul Klee wrote

There is only one true thing.

In the Self

a small

stone.

I remember my own
act of registry.

So you would not call it the seed.

And Olson
said
in I think his Berkeley lecture
That the earth is just a big stone
and he of course had seen the glacial deposits
and the solid beach of stones at Pigeon Cove.

This is one of the things I thought about
this fact of there being so many
heavy stones
at Pigeon Cove
one day when my brother
Tony came to visit me
and I was living in Gloucester
near Eastern Point
that summer

and had come upon a terrible thing
in seeing gelatinous creatures
of the inlet
that they would survive if the sun did not
dry up the little pool
in which they conducted their struggle
before the next tide

and that the gulls always
when they sat in the afternoon
on Crane's Beach
or at Good Harbor Beach
seemed to be facing landward

I thought there is something
that wants to last a very long time

or to cast itself in such a process
at least in part
that it should last

and that these stones were in part
the success of such a process

and that we as persons were of a like success

and I had already written at that time
though thinking to mean something different by it

we may be
that stone

A POSSIBILITY

A POSSIBILITY

you can watch
the moon
every night

but can you watch
the changes
in the deity
of the moon

do the greatest poets get their powers from pacts

or do they gain these powers
of breaking pacts
with infinite circumspection

sufficient earth
in love with powers of air

are there spirits who use poets

all the beauty men ever believed
is perhaps the power
of what they are

and all the terror that men do

come from the pacts
other men make with them

perhaps in secreted deeps of self

whole communities
        quite possibly
                        serve
energies
        emergent
                    here and there

this people facets its city thus

their architectonics

their modes of time

the face that such a deity wears upon them

for some cause it has

the sibyl
over the fault

keeping the magnetized apparatus thus
                              only
these shapes are so

and certain old brain
possibilities
are not otherwise active than
by animal sacrifice

what will you do
if the deity prove to inhabit
the persons of
your most remote
bad dreams

or there is something working
in your own desire
                    not
clear to you

isn't it true that to
be a
man is
more than this

and isn't it
among the truths
not known
if
someone says he knows
it shows who
he is

how a man is
more than this

noble spirit

rise
in the inner courts
or nowhere

I don't want to have to see you on T.V.

pleased to greet you

this man's magic will not
easily
work for you

no one man can
take upon
himself another's will

and it is not a good thing for any man
so to mistrust himself

though there are those who counterwork
the consequent of
such working

their offices
can be purchased

their purchase
can be used

if you have made a pact

and wish to break it

and the gangs in your aura are loud

The demon is not   but metaphorically so
                                        though
operant upon such clutches of homology
as our metaphors
                    are
                        they
ride the storms of men
                            we
see them
in the lives of our friends as
they
        in turn
                    perceive them
in our lives
                or
        more fearfully
in their own

others may go
                not wakefully
impercipient
                of the larger
strides their own steps move among
                                    taking
the dailiness
as needful
of no more regard

even what pass as
the best of men may
live thus humbled
by others'
purposes

and those most conversant
in these matters
all the more
are used

        who
speaks in me

that I am only myself
participated by my own possession

I ride a fruited cloud

the danger

only our occasion

and the desire

that pulls the eye

along the page

faster

to get to the part

where the ally is less

than we are

or where the listener

penetrates the vault

and there is a goddess

painted on the bottom of

sarcophagi

remembering that to die

sings in every fear

there is no monstrum

more than this